Lone Prairie

By Bill Buege

Published by Burlesque Press

Lone Prairie

Book design by Daniel Wallace
Cover image by Steel Bokhof
Burleseque Press

No part of this publication may be reproduced, stored in a retrieval system or transmitted in any way by any means, electronic, mechanical, photocopy, recording or otherwise without the prior permission of the author except as provided by USA copyright law.

ISBN: 978-1-735035-1-3

Bill Buege
7270 Princeton, University City, MO 63130 USA
bbuege117@gmail.com
Phone: 1-314-726-0699

Published in the United States of America
Publication date: May 2024

Dedication

For my daughters, Amanda Boyden, Margaret Greteman, and Emily Bihun. And for their mother, Sandra.

Table of Contents

Lone Prairie	4
Uncle Buckley	5
Silent Night	6
Donna	7
Sunfish and Sandy	8
In-laws	9
Loretta and Theron	10
County Lock Up	11
Fairgrounds: Three Guns	12
Surplus Commodities	13
The Man with Half a Face	14
A Farm Woman	15
Ted	16
Acting Pastor	17
Lone Prairie Fun	18
Women	19
Bob, Julia, Bill	20
A Comet and a Tornado	21
No Electric, No Plumbing	22
Snow	23
Cheap	24
Woke	25
Smelt	26
A Gift	27
Street Tennis	28
Gordy and Carol	29
So He	30
My Life on the Mississippi	32
Bad Dentist Minneapolis spring, 1947	33
Minneapolis summer, 1960	35
Minneapolis 1963	37
Minneapolis winter, 1999	39
A Visit	39

St. Louis spring 1970	41
St Louis summer, 1985	43
St. Louis Autumn 2015-2020	45
St. Louis winter, 2022	46
New Orleans, 2010, Spring	47
New Orleans July, any summer	49
New Orleans Autumn 2005	51
NOLA Winter, January-March, 2014	53
The Light (coda)	55
Guaranteed	57
It Will Never Happen	58
Everything Is Alive	59
A Sweet for January 1	61
Why Do They Insist	62
Boundary Waters Song	64
January Thursday	65
Asparagus	67
She Dances	69
A Few Lines for Daisy	70
A Widower and a Linden Tree	71
Mozart's Birthday	72
Old Man Shoveling Snow	73
Old Man Makes Dinner for Himself	74
And for His Dog	75
Old Man Ventures Out	76
Old Man Reads His Old Testament	77
What an Old Man Thinks Funny	78
Old Man's Bedtime Checklist	79
What an Old Man Fears	80
What an Old Man Fears Most	82
Two Missouri Gardens, an Old Man, a Child	84

BOOKS PUBLISHED

Jill: a poem in 100 Spenserian stanzas (Tamafyhr Mountain Press, 2007)

Imitations (Chiron Review Press, 2008)

Stumble Into a Lighted Room (Burlesque Press, 2016)

In Their Time (Burlesque Press, 2020)

"Gentle breath of yours my sails
Must fill or else my project fails,
Which was to please."

(The Tempest, Epilogue ls. 11--13)

Section I.

Lone Prairie

Section I

LONE PRAIRIE

Once upon a time there was a little town in central Minnesota,
And once upon a time a man was twenty-three, a new husband,
First time employee, new intake worker at the county welfare office.

Once twenty-five hundred mostly poor people lived, worked,
Fished, cooked, grew there, died in the little hospital, celebrated
At the fairgrounds, bowled, bought dishwashers, rifles from the one

Hardware store, ate at the diner on Main. A new baby, a girl, born
There September Third cost her parents fifty dollars for the doctor,
One hundred fifty more for the hospital. The doctor told the wife,

Well along in labor, to walk the hall a bit to speed the birth. The child
Was named Amanda, the father, Bill, the mother, Sandra. They lived
In a little white frame house, drove a little old green Mercury Comet,

Enjoyed the quiet, the new life as adults, their baby. Once upon a time
The sun shone every day in Lone Prairie; the snow, when it came,
Fell silent, beautiful, white; the breeze brought winter wood smoke,

Summer green, fall farmland harvests. And every evening a group
Of employees from the welfare office gathered at the little white house,
Talked, laughed, fell in love with one another. Life was very fine,

Fresh, new in Lone Prairie, Minnesota, long ago, once upon a time.

Uncle Buckley

(In memory of E Buckley Glabe: 1899-1969)

Alcoholic, famous early welfare
Mind, onetime cowboy, preacher, carried
A revolver to seminary, spent

His final days at his kitchen table
Drinking vodka, reading. He and Bill's Dad
Played general and aide in local bars,

Worried the drunks. Buckley influenced
Minnesota welfare. They owed him.
He paved a straight road for young Bill

Lone Prairie

Silent Night

Twenty-five miles from Lindbergh's Little Falls
To tiny Lone Prairie. A thick black night, black road,
Two young adults hushed in the emptiness

Too dark for city folk. Alone. No signs.
No traffic. Their little car. A county road.
When above them they hear a stereo rush of sound,

Fueled, sudden, across the starless sky.
A flash of light. They have no words for this,
Their headlight tunnel, new lives, silent night.

Donna

A real job, real small town, real folk.
He moved his pregnant wife, bed, books,
A hundred miles north. It would work

This time. No more grad school. It looked
Like a sweet little place. He'd help
The poor. The good folk would like

Him. Donna sure did, picked him up
On her motorcycle. His dick woke
When she shouted, Want to fuck? Yep.

Lone Prairie

Sunfish and Sandy

She, eight months pregnant, sweating
On the kitchen floor, cleaning sunfish,
A bucket of them. An August catch

Hauled home from a farm lake paradise.
Her husband wanted to fish. Twelve miles east,
Turn south on the dirt road, knock.

He'll rent you a small boat. Row to the bay
Filled with wild rice. Use worms. You'll catch
A rainbow platter of glittering gold.

In-laws

For him she was the Christ child, born
Perfect, a bit of heaven, total
Joy, the future. His heart was torn

From his chest when she, as all
Newborns do, held his finger, smiled.
You promised her the best, not this shit hole,

Grandma, drunk, raged. To calm her, they played
Cribbage. He tried to lose, won and won
Till, Hit him, Frank, the nut case yelled.

Lone Prairie

Loretta and Theron

A fine woman, best boss he'd ever have,
She ran the office, smoked constantly,
Wore full skirts, patterned dresses, loved

The poor, her work, her life, her employees.
A plain, delightful woman. Husband Theron,
Second in command, smoked, smiled, free,

It seemed, from stress, cared for. He'd won
The lottery when he married her. She gave
Him strength, position, grace, herself, her town.

County Lock Up

The new intake worker walked into the cell.
Emotionless, a pale young man sat staring
At nothing. How are you? Dumb. You well?

Dumber. How can I help? Dumbest. Willing
To do most anything, was told to drive the guy
Out of the county, give him ten bucks, thus, sparing

The local court, jail, system, county good name. My
God, I'm to let this guy in my car. He could kill
Me. No. Here's a ten. Do your job. Good luck. Bye.

Lone Prairie

Fairgrounds: Three Guns

1.
He'd never owned a weapon, but, then,
He'd never married, either, never
Had a fulltime job. Bought a Remington

Pump-action twenty-two, scoped, for
Half his monthly salary He loved its feel,
Took it, long-rifle shells, his wire haired terrier

To the fairground, set a tin can on a hill,
Blew it full of holes, almost shot his dog when
Foxy ran barking at the can, crazy for the kill.

2.
Friend Dave Dodd had real fire power,
Carried a forty-five, leftover from
World War Two, scrubbed clean, greased, pure

American goodness, polished chrome.
Fired heavy, went thump, thump, thump. Not bang.
Erection, he-man stuff. The heirloom

Snugged into the hand. The lead whanged
Through the can. The shooter's grip remembered
The thump after he forgot most things.

3.
Brother-in-law brought a Browning shotgun
North to town. They drove to the fairgrounds,
Hauled a hand thrower, clay pigeons,

Blasted away. A miracle, the virgin
Shooter shattered ten in a row.
He'd never shot a twelve gauge. Later, gone

Home, he rubbed his right shoulder. Swollen (Ow!),
Bruised. Must not have held it tight. Come on,
He'd brought down one, two, ... ten. Just so.

Surplus Commodities

Once a month he handed them
Half-gallon cans of peanut butter.
The others gave out rice, flour, jam,

Beans, milk, all with a smile. Better
This than paperwork. All day
The people came, carrying their

Cardboard boxes, stood patiently
In line. He saw they needed him,
He, them, their toughness, certainly.

Lone Prairie

THE MAN WITH HALF A FACE

He drove into the woods, deep, dark,
Hansel and Gretel nightmare, found
The house, finally knocked. A streak

Of light (yah, yah, I'm coming) showed round
The door. A man with half a face
Came out. "I'm from the welfare." He frowned,

Grunted. "We'll drive to Mayo." His nose
Was gone, most of his lips, chin, cheeks,
He lit a smoke in the empty space.

A Farm Woman

1.
They told him they'd tried to get in, but the farmer swore
He'd shotgun them, released his dogs. They ran.
The new man said he'd go. No dogs. The front door

Locked. No farmer. He knocked. A raggedy woman,
Frightened, peeked out. He pushed past her. The hall
Was covered with garbage. He slid across to the kitchen.

All rooms were matted with filth and decay. Two small
Boys, a dog, ate food scraps off the floor.
A girl smeared her shit on a dining room wall

2.
It took a month, a half dozen cleaning women.
Welfare removed the children from the home.
Plastic bags of waste filled three garbage bins.

The farmer vanished into his own gloom.
Four dogs were euthanized. The deeper problems,
Cruelty, isolation, helplessness, no crumb

Of worth, were whitewashed. They fit her in their dream:
Pancake makeup, clean clothes, new coat, robin
Orange lipstick, permed hair. Now, she looked like them.

Lone Prairie

TED

City boy stuck in a county welfare
Department, drives to Saint Paul weekends
To carouse, ends up in the slammer

Or the locked psych ward, where he stands
Staring, drugged, last we see him through
A steel door window. Weekdays, our friend

Preaches, No matter what you do
Or say, (Oh, Ted) I'm still [sober]
A worthwhile person. Our sweet cuckoo.

Acting Pastor

Amen. Yes, he'd done it, led a service,
Read the liturgy, sermon, Sunday prayers.
Put on the pastor's vestments, took his place.

After being kicked from the seminary!
He'd matured, learned to care. Ready
To serve. To bury his pride. He might just dare

Go back. The hundred small town souls in their Sunday
Pews froze at her shout, "You didn't pray for my Thomas.
Damn you." Her anger ended his fantasy.

Lone Prairie Fun

The fairgrounds touted a fenced-in softball field,
Slow-pitch league of fat store owners, printing
Press employees, farmers, the bowling team's

One young welfare fella. College boy, just north
Of dumb. Nice looking wife, though. The men
Drank brandy, smoked cheap cigars, watched him

Strike out three games in a row. Let him hit one.
Hank floated it. The league's joke took aim, swung,
Connected. Way over the fence. Not that fat, Hank.

Buege

WOMEN

Wherever he went there were women,
And he was twenty-three, tall, fairly strong,
Friendly. Too friendly. His father had been

Friendly, too. Too friendly, his mother said.
Even at eighty-five, which would be years
Later. His new little town was at least

Half women. Women who smiled, dreamed,
Thought of what he thought of day and night.
Married, widowed, young, old. Ah, me.

Lone Prairie

Bob, Julia, Bill

Julia worked aid for children and single
Mothers. Bob handled the complex cases,
Married, up from the Twin Cities,

Owned a house on a nearby lake, wasn't
Going anywhere. The small town life
Was his life. Julia, older, single, befriended

Young Bill, was told to make him a pro,
Took him to Sauk Centre, Sinclair Lewis' home.
Bill fancied himself a poet, not a caretaker.

A Comet and a Tornado

He drove an old green Comet up and down
The county visiting farms, the elderly,
And a nursing home where an old lady

Pounded holes in her door with her cane,
Everything smelled of shit. One morning
Driving north to Staples, he looked off

To the east at an enormous black cone drilling
Into the earth, spitting dust, rushing at him.
He floored his Comet, heard the passing roar.

No Electric, No Plumbing

Loretta asked him to visit a farm,
A couple in their eighties. It's getting cold.
Sure. Their little low-roofed house was warm.

They seemed people from a book, both small,
Both dressed in clean old clothes, both content.
They had no money. He offered them welfare.

Thank you, but no. You're sure? Yes, we're fine.
We have each other, our home, can manage
On our own. Perplexed, he drove back to town.

Snow

They told him of farmers who went out
To feed their cattle, lost their way,
Were found in spring melt, popsicles, not

Unhappy, content seeming, maybe
Aware they no longer need drudge
Their way through a rough life, sorry

Soil, cow shit, bitter wife. Townsfolk gauged
Snowfall by farmhouse walls. "You ought
Watch yourself out there." No, he'd manage.

Lone Prairie

Cheap

They bought it cheap, freedom, barn, fields, house,
Moved from Chicago's north side, used the last
Of their savings for a small herd of milk cows.

They knew nothing of farming, dreamed harvests,
Ignored the animals, hard work. The children deviled
The cows, the dogs. The man recalled the taste

Of failure. Fall brought freeze, stasis. They filled
Their stove with green elm, burned their choices,
The herd starved in the filthy stalls, lay still.

WOKE

Baby Amanda's crying woke him at two.
Why was it so cold? Twenty-five
Below outside, fifty in. What now?

He muttered, dressed, went downstairs.
Out of fuel oil. God damn it. His fault.
He woke his wife, bundled Amy, drove them

To Gordy and Carol's, drove off, distraught
(Did not know to take care. A dog would know),
Found an open station, kindness, heat.

Lone Prairie

SMELT

The Lone Prairie bowling team decided
To go night fishing in Lake Superior,
Coaxed along the new man, citified, red-eyed,

Worried he'd drown in the unforgiving water.
They parked by a still, small bay (ice chunks floated
On its midnight surface), unloaded their

Brandy, well-used nets, waders, hats, coats, scouted
The shore, waded in up to their waists, netted
Six milk cans of smelt, drove home blottoed.

A Gift

April, the snow began to melt.
Toward the end of the month,
The ground woke. Come May,

Lilac breath drifted across
The backyard. A few tough weeds
Poked from the grass.

And spears of something
Barely visible clustered
Behind the little frame house.

A gift from a renter? Notice:
We survived another
Minnesota winter. Asparagus.

Lone Prairie

STREET TENNIS

Drifts edge their street. They wear sweaters,
Drag out their rackets, tennis balls,
Wrap Amanda snug in her stroller,

Set her by the curb. Ready. All
Imagined: net, court, famous players.
He is handsome Newcombe, tall,

Strong, she, Virginia Wade. The neighbors
Watch from draped windows, wonder
What next? City folk. Dumb and dumber.

Gordy and Carol

Came over every night with Dave,
A couple others, drank, talked. Gordy
Lusted for Sandra but was married

To Carol, who preferred Bill, who loved
Being preferred. Dave loved his guns
And diary. Gordy worked at Welfare,

Had been accepted at the U of M
For his MSW, which made Bill jealous.
They were young, eager, blind to their fates.

Lone Prairie

So He

Wasn't going to be outdone by Gordy,
Was accepted at Valpo for a useless MA,
Packed up his wife and daughter, found

A cattle truck that would move them
To Indiana cheap. Off they went, away
From their one good thing, headed for

An intellectual life. Fate watched and shook
Her head, another story of the young fool
Leaving the best he'd ever have. Boring.

Section II

My Life on the Mississippi

Now, don't get me wrong. I never piloted a steamboat on the old girl, nor, for that matter, floated on a barge, canoe, log like the roughnecks Huckleberry swam to. I've lived a life (stretching out a bit, it seems), pretty durn close to the old woman, crawled her banks, sling-shotted cherry bombs above her, crept across her under the old Lake Street bridge, hiked Minnehaha's runoff, heaved rocks at the carp, but I ain't ever been out on her. Oh, except once we ate dinner on a docked riverboat. So, here's me, a boy in Minneapolis, grownup (sort of, somewhat, tried, at least) in St. Louis, soiled snowbird on a bench in New Orleans, watching the giant ships push by from all parts of the planet, imagining me turned corpse, a joyful tote in a parade down Magazine. I'm not shooting for complexity, profundity, thoroughness, just for a cheese Whopper, fries, and a coke. Aw, shucks, I admit I might have imagined a little. Hope you enjoy a bite or two.

Bad Dentist Minneapolis Spring, 1947

A panicked child, a little boy,
Races down Lyndale Ave, pursued
By an angry man in whites.

Clear sky fresh, lilac sweet, quiet
Under budding elms, new life,
New boy, war veteran father,

Servant mother. Your gift boy's
Future. He has seventy-five
Or eighty more years to live,

Unless the white coated man
Turns cruel, the boy is struck
By that new black Plymouth.

What will happen when they drag
The reckless child back, strap him
To a chair, turn on the gas,

Prop open his mouth? He won't
Know the risks, wakes, goes home,
Never forgets he had free will.

He decided. He leapt up, ran
Past the receptionist, out the door.
He decided. He did it. Will never

Again be so bold, so certain
Of what he wanted. Sad that
The kid surrendered, broken,

Lone Prairie

Became a devious teen. Spring
Sun shone. Sweet lilacs bloomed.
Hitler lay dead from suicide.

The boy's father, a war hardened
Army captain, knew how to shape
Privates, ruled with a fighter's hand.

Minneapolis summer, 1960

Out of Control

1.
The arrow bounced off the bleachers
Two feet above (he'd dropped) his head.
Missed him, but good try. This preacher

School and I don't fit, and I'm fed
Up with the Bible, Hebrew, Greek.
Bores me stiff. Gary could be dead,

Bob chokes. Well, I aimed for his neck.
You're crazy. Could be a teacher.
But you like guns. What's not to like?

2.
Almost got that rabbit. Fucker
Ducked out of my headlights. You made
Car tracks across the quad. Liquor

Hypes me. Can't get stuck here. I'm dead
If they catch me. What if someone's
Making out? Fuck them. You need God.

God doesn't care. We're his ants, His fun
Watching us fuck up. You're sicker
Than I thought. Think I'll buy a gun.

3.
ADHD? Not in those days.
After school we hitch a ride home,
Hop in a back seat. Man says,

Lone Prairie

You're cute little guys. You want some
Special candy? Oh, no, bad ride.
Driver turns, looks at me. I'll come

On the big ones face once he's dead.
Red light. Leap out! Holy shit, guess
I'm not the craziest. Thank God!

Minneapolis 1963

Falling Apart

1.
He failed Hebrew twice, refused to go to class.
They refused to graduate him without it.
The classic standoff. Summers he'd worked his ass

Off on a road crew. Not now. He has to bite
His tongue, conform, take two four week all day,
Pass or enlist, bub, Sem level classes. Git

Down an do it, his old man yelled; so he
Learned to read the Pentateuch just as
It was writ, upside down. Oh, man, oh my.

2.
Passed. Solved nothing. Thought he'd escaped, but they
Caught their nigger in the swamp, chained him. Sect
Time for you, Bud. Soon you'll see God. All day

They yelled at him. Dogmatics, homiletics,
Hermeneutics, aorists, schwas, inerrancy.
He got a night job parking cars. Intellects

Aren't meant for this, bought a fifth, Beam. I see
My route out, earn a minus GPA.
Son, we'll pray for ya. Give Dad our best. Bye.

3.
Off he goes back home. Kid's nuts. Treat him
With care. What now? Viet Nam? Naw. Married
A pretty young thing. Big wedding. A shame

Lone Prairie

He's not smart like his Dad. Kid's nuts, can't hide
It, poor wife. Gets in grad school, U of Minn.,
Philosophy, switches to psych, young bride

At home. He flourishes. She's bored, alone.
He excels, reborn. Statistics, two-man game
Theory. Listen! She's bored. He quits. Hell wins.

Minneapolis Winter, 1999
A Visit

1.
He Accused Me
I'll name names. He's dead awhile.
Ray Gierke, her parents' friend, good
Church man. We'd divorced, evil

Per Ray. Pastor's son's fault. "Should"
Ruled Ray's life. Hello, Ray. You look
Good. You hurt her. What? You could

Have worked things out. What? You took
Her everything. Later, Ray. I'll
Walk up, greet pastor. We'll talk.

2.
Where?
Christ Church, Minneapolis. I'd
Driven six hundred miles to see
What shaped me. Old me always lied:

Gifted as few are, I owned me,
Could fail and fail yet never fall.
Even here, I was time's pea. Ray

Remembered me. Wow! Might it all
Work out? Had I escaped my bed,
My brick shit house, cleaned my stable?

3.
Yes, It Was
Beautiful. Saarinen's creation,
Winter morning light, God's presence, hush

Lone Prairie

Of good and true, my gift, redemption

Of a fucked up life. No need to push
Myself into prominence. I could
Thrive, blessed by the peace in Eliel's church.

Redeemed Bill, reborn in light, swaddled
In holy silence, grows wings. Soul shine
Quickly fades. I drove home, re-addled.

St. Louis spring 1970

1.
Why Go Here?
Why anywhere? St. Louis, an odd
Choice. Bad prof, be gone. College needs you not.
You failed, sir. He rented a truck (God

Must have sent an angel), drove about
As badly as most things he did. He can't
Find his way. He has children. The lout

Once wrote a note to them, "Goodbye. Don't
Look for me. I won't be there," Free, he rode
Away. Meg begged, Daddy, I know you won't.

2.
He Lied
Almost died that night. Dream pills, weeks off,
Finished the quarter, said good-byes, packed, left
For something, anything. Found enough,

Copy editor job, sweet, Dad's gift
To his church. Prodigal son did not know
Caesar from Ceasar. Professional proofed,

Caught it. Dope was transferred. This is how
Business works, the fuck-up thought. Sure is tough
To get ahead wherever you go.

3.
But Didn't Leave St. Louis
He'd left several lives, his children, good wife,
A shooting gallery of jobs, he found
Psych help, a new spouse, MBA, new life.

Lone Prairie

Love dawned on him. No quitting. Shrink bound
Him to gratitude, perseverance, all
He wanted but in better ways. He learned

To forgive (shrink gift), hired to overhaul
Surveillance, enjoyed his work, his life, knifed
His father's faith demands. And he grew tall.

St Louis summer, 1985

1.
New Wife
She'd lived a bit longer, marooned in the land
Of middle age, drank, smoked, New Jersey born,
Moved west with her rich, abusive husband,

A drunk, divorced him when her sib, his gun,
FBI special, out, said, "She's leaving."
That was that. A dark eyed beauty, she'd run

A little wild, liked wealth. He, still grieving
For his lost family, poor, naïve, seemed bound
For hell. Or not. Both needed forgiving

2.
New Job
He wept at their wedding. My God, she thought,
What have I done? But their bond held, and they,
Slowly, fell in love. She quit smoking. Ought

To stop gin. I'll switch to wine. He's too fay;
We'll fix that. He grew, stuck at work, liked it.
Summers, she drove with him. He did not cry

As often. No more a boy-man. A bit
Timid for her taste and his job. He caught
Cheats, stock hustlers, thought himself a poet.

3.
New Children
She harried him sore, her lips a snarl.
Her two must want not, no, may not
Be bothered. Battered, he conceded;

Lone Prairie

His Cinderellas left for their dance.
Her daughter moved to the street,
Sold drugs, herself. Her son knew he

Was Thor, the man; his mother's worn dildo,
Discardable. The daughter's life sputtered.
The wife refused to let her grown child die.

St. Louis Autumn 2015-2020

The Limits of Retirement

One day she backed into the neighbor's car.

One day, driving home from her hairdresser, she lost her way.

One day she went for a walk near her home. A young couple found her wandering, helped her back.

One day she failed her memory test. The social worker told him she must not drive. Tears blurred his eyes.

One day she came downstairs with her skirt over her head.

One day she was blind, another day, deaf.

One day she spoke with him by putting his finger in her mouth.

One day the nurse told him she had turned a corner.

One day the following week, she died.

St. Louis winter, 2022

Paranoia Blues

Did he with her? Did she with him, that one,
When we vacationed in Hawaii years
Ago, before her illness? Who cares? They're gone,
Ensconced in history. And me? My dear,
It tickles me in my old age, to think
My second wife had that much joy. We lived
Lovebird lives, it seemed. Lubricious mink
Cannot be blamed for what they are. Forgive?
What right have I? You did not worry me,
Your cuckold. Eager, naïve, I did not know
You well, was warned off you, your family.
Innate wildness, dark eyes, nice butt. Go slow,
Anyone but her. He married them.
Forty years ignorant! I love you. Damn.

New Orleans, 2010, Spring

Alone

1.
Fly loafer on a bench at peace
With the Mississippi, myself,
Waiting for a great ship to pass

Empty, downstream, out to the Gulf,
Upstream, fighting the hard current,
Stern foreign flags blowing. I wolf

My oyster po boy, sweet sun sent
Air kissed for old Bill, notice
Two toughs, pit bull, see me. Run? Can't.

2.
Casual, easy boys approach,
Stand over bichon Fang, me, smile.
Snakes. Where you from? Fang growls. I belch.

Sorry. Love fried oysters. I'm full,
Your dog want the rest? Scared? Just stuffed.
Pit bulls love their owners. Awhile

Ago almost shot one. Enough
Violence in our world. I reach
Back, grin. They walk on, buy my bluff.

3.
Best jog over, flirt with the girls
Tanning in the NOLA sun. Joke?
I'd be the joke, the creep, the smell

Lone Prairie

On their blanket. I have the coke.
You have the skin, the eyes, the smile.
Let's have fun. Love to, but we're broke.

My fantasy. College kids! I'll
Move on, stare (old yuck). Pit bull,
Toughs? Let him be. He's weak, senile.

New Orleans July, any summer

This Ain't the Garden District

The old roach takes shade under
The leaking sink,

Space the millipede calls home.
The two cool, or try.

The rats sleep deep
As the sewers lead.

We lie in our underwear
On sheets wet with our sweat,

Hypnotized by the ceiling fan
And sun bogged time.

We know where not to be--
Out there, where sun

Has bleached the sky, blistered
The paint on the stair railing.

Between out there, in here,
The shutters leak slices of sun.

The worn fan thrums,
Says what we choose to hear,

Today is your day to do nothing,
Lie still, forget sex, breathe.

Lone Prairie

The fan knows time will
Hand heat to night

While it creaks on,
We try for a little sleep.

New Orleans Autumn 2005

1.
And Then
A few drops, warnings, sky lowers, greys.
Aw, shucks. Again? We be fine. It can't.
Magazine, St. Charles, Lasalle, hey,

Can't be, they be rivers. No, we ain't
Gonna leave. We here since we be born.
Ma, Gran can't get out. Bro cut hole. Aunt

Go under wid baby Joe. I watch drown.
They ghost, howl wid wind. Dome shit-filthy,
Rape, murder, end time time. Ninth ward gone.

2.
And
Asthma, can't breathe here, can't get out
In air, gotta find one hole, pray
This roof is rotten. Been about

Thirty years since he laid it, way
Long enough. That cheap tar paper
Gone holey, and termites chew day

And night. Dear God, stay by me here.
Old and worn, I don't complain, ain't
Worth much round those mansions up there.

3.
Floating
Free at last. Goodbye Yes sir, shutten
Up, free to be me, little boy again
On the river. Ole spring sun shinen

Lone Prairie

Down on a happy kid like I win
The teddy at the fair. Man, sure feel good,
Might could do this days. Can't feel nuthin,

No matter. Old catfish in no mood
Say hello, turtle nod. Somethin biten
me, seem. Don't hurt none. Nothin's bad

NOLA Winter, January-March, 2014

1.
A Block Off Magazine

My paradise? Better. It's real
Or appears to me to be. Don't want more,
Need more, deserve more than I feel

This moment in my time. Sunshine pours
Drafts of hellos, mixed-folk walkers, beer can
Waves, Le Bon Temps Roule` their bar,

Goal. My goal? Sit on this porch, sun
Lit, content as sun-warmed geckoes, until
Day hands night her blues, his saxophone.

2.
Sunday Morning

Wallace owns it, I know, but, listen, we
Walked through sunshine as if the sun loved us,
Kissed our toes, said, "Worship well. I grant thee

An hour of high church holiness, its peace,
Afterward, my Garden District flowers
Above your heads, NOLA quiet, obese,

Hanging fruit you dare not pick, forever
Memories, thick ice creams, my panoply
Of earth's delights, for you, this Sunday, here."

Lone Prairie

3.
Parade

He's stunned by the St. Patrick's beauties, each
Fantasy a way to blur the day's mobs.
Stoned moms, their sugar stupefied kids stretch

Prayerful arms for junk, beads, oh, please. Gods lob
Booty, bless beggars from float heights. Twenties
Girls raise T's teasing. His giddy wife, robbed

By dementia, shouts, begs, terribly
Focused, walks off, arms full, lost. He will search
Blocks for her. Let her be. She's so happy.

The Light (coda)

1.
Apart from a planet, our world, our eyes,
The light has nothing to attach itself.
On through empty space at its own speed,
The maximum speed, it wanders,
Curves on its track, searching, searching.

2.
Apart from a planet, debris, comet, the light
Has nothing to avoid, nothing to impede
Its joy filled race through the universal
Night. Darkness cannot contain it.

3.
Given the nature of the universe,
The light may race on alive forever.

4.
Darkness gloats on the stuff it swallows.

Section III

Guaranteed

They will pick up the bowl
Remember how proud he was to have made it

They will recite what he said about ... Who?

What he said about, I forget his name, but ...
And how he tried to get them to talk about their day

They will joke about the relief they feel
At not having to eat his baked salmon

Gradually, they will forget

As they go about their week
As years pass
As they grow old

You know what today is?
The day Daddy died
Hard to believe six years ago

I remember once when I was in high school ...
Yes, I think about those days, too

It Will Never Happen

He's going to live forever
She gets worse so slowly
Day after day she stays the same
How long ago
Was she first diagnosed?
How old is he?

Inconsiderate time
Ignores the dog's death,
The baby's birth, christening
Family marriages

The no longer new house
Expensive to keep up

The man and the woman hang on
And on
And then they don't

And before you know it,
Christmas laps the calendar
The couple divorce
The baby starts high school

Everything Is Alive

1.
My pills hang out in the bottom
Of their bottles, push their timid neighbors
To the top. They love their freedom,

Temporary though it is. Scores
Of antique words work their way deep inside
My brain, giggle while I labor

To find the one right word, play hide
And seek until I squeeze one out, feel dumb
As a log. Log groans, "I abide."

2.
We recognize one another.
Wasn't always so. I smashed a rock in half,
Threw garden dust in the water,

Made cool mud. Brad farted. I laughed
As the stench drifted on the air. Little
Did life's extent move us, wrapped safe

In ignorance. The State whittled
At the truths we could know. We can't bother
Children with facts. "Fine," sings Kettle.

3.
If all live, all die. I figured that out
Without the help of history, itself
Alive, dead, resurrected, about

Lone Prairie

What is, what was, what may be. The pols' wolf
Bangs on my door, History implies we
May lose white purity. Christ, himself,

Was white. We must be sure children will die
Unaware of dust, mud, air. Better not
Feed them fish. "Right on," gurgles Mud Pie.

A Sweet for January 1

In the beginning
The beginning passed
Became shortly after the beginning,

A little longer, but not much,
Maybe because one tires from too much separation.
I, for one, am one with the crowds clinging to their beds.

Which is all I have, but not what you
Or you or you have, or my great grandfather had,
A tough guy with his minutes, too.

Granted, it is the second day and way too warm
For here, but not unexpected.
We need something to worry about.

Face it, we've made something to worry about.
For ourselves, our brood.
Forgive us this day. And yesterday.

My daughter made me toffee for Christmas.
I suck on a piece for a while, bite down on it,
Cannot open my mouth. Love it.

Why Do They Insist

That I become involved?
Look, I'm pretty old, daily
Older, tout a walking stick

Limp, melanoma, iffy
Heart, lungs, have become
A hermit, but what I read

Insists that politics has gone
To shit and I must worry,
Help fix America. Why must

I care? I want to imagine
A healthy prostate, French
Fries, burgers at McDs,

A chubby, happy, lubricious
Young wife, wasted days
Writing, fucking, fiddling

In the market. Made a few
Bucks once. Intoxicating!
Quit when I saw my bucks

Vanish into fancier pockets.
I'm ready to disappear.
Nothingness calls, Hey, Bill.

Then, I learn I must look
Back to the Fifties when
White men rode white horses,

Buege

Kids hid under their desks
So the atomic bombs would
Not kill them. Kids grew

Into crooked, crazy senators,
Willful liars, ingenious myth
Makers, thank God, died.

Boundary Waters Song

She's videoed fresh against a background
Of Minnesota north, black coffee, lakes,
Ragweed, watermelon, her good legs, round

Swimsuit molded butt, clipped blond hair. She takes
My breath, dry eyes, fingers. Stranded outside
Her reality, staring, near heartbreak,

I would be hers, live for her, satisfied
By her songs of single pleasure, her good
Life, youth, voice, my fantasy, deified.

January Thursday

I'm home. No women come and go
Talking of Michelangelo,

Winslow Homer, Jeopardy.
I've escaped suits for paternity.

Last night glass fell from my front door.
Ding dong dell, oh, well. What more?

It rang the neighbors like cellphones.
No one answered. I heard the groans,

Don't bother me's. Women won't return
My calls. For them I burn,

Offend, read I must cut it off.
Like hell. Enough.

I hear a what? A knock, a Visigoth
Roof salesman. I am wroth

To answer since no lady cometh forth,
Not here, no one for me, worth-

Less, basted, almost done, a little rare.
I have no hair,
Wear the elastic in my underwear

Accidently rolled.
I've grown old,

Lone Prairie

Dare not eat fish,
A mercury poisoned dish.
I see the far shore bright and clear,
Rushing near.

Asparagus

Hush, dear, they'll hear,
Throw us into the wild weeds,
Where we won't last a bleak

While. What is a while anyway?
I think about awhile while
From time to time I sprout.

There's that thing again, time.
Oh, I know, it's not a thing,
It's something else, but if it is,

It's got to be something.
Honey bunch, I'm lost. Watch out
For those tomato plants,

Greedy feeders, sneakers,
Vitamin gobblers! And pumpkin
Vines! The evil creepers.

Before one little season, you're
Overrun and die, while they
Make their fat orange fruit.

If their orange stink plops on you,
The berserkers save the great plop,
Ignore gasping you. People,

Rootless vegetables! Sweet sprout,
Learn from corn plants. They grow
Huge, princes, they think. Wait.

Down they fall in fall. Ha, ha.

Lone Prairie

Yes, the lard heads clip us, too, but
Our best part snugs deep in loam.

Here comes the frantic one.
She has her pail and spade.
Poor potatoes! Glad we're not.

She Dances

Her lunch hour all music,
Her crinolines flying, eyes on fire,
High school girls laughing,

She is too beautiful for then,
That place, that time, too alive
At seventeen, blessed with grace.

At eighty-three, quietly, blind,
Deaf, she dies. An aid has brushed
Her hair. She lies on her side.

Freed, she dances, sparkles,
Laughs at me on the sidelines
In my time, in her evernow.

A Few Lines for Daisy

Little white dog,
My sister found you
Shaking in the corner

Of your cell. You were
Dog years old, had few
Teeth, lived unwanted,

A ball of dirty hair.
Loss blurred your eyes.
Karen is a sucker

For helplessness, took
You home, made you
Into her beautiful friend.

For a few months,
You raced about
Her backyard.

Your eyes woke,
But your problems
Could not be fixed.

We die. It's what we are,
Animals that die, but
For a while, we get to be

Animals that live,
Race about backyards,
Love little, helpless things.

Buege

A Widower and a Linden Tree

Yesterday's rain slowed
To mist, and in agreement
With night and the universe

Wrapped my linden tree in ice.
This morning she insists
I stare at her proud nakedness

Beneath her wintry couture.
Warm summer days she fills
My backyard with her gown.

I put two chairs, our little table
Under her, late May mornings
Sit alone beneath my tree. I am

Don Corleone by his tomato plants.
She is my companion. My linden,
Grown strong, watches over me.

Mozart's Birthday

How difficult to comprehend a human with such talent.
Even from the distance of my ignorance, I accept
The gift of one that far above the rest of us. Snow

Pours on Saint Louis today. It was to be half an inch,
But we already have four times that much but how
The weather people have improved. Yesterday, a man

Delivered groceries to my front door. Cost more,
Twice as much as I would pay, normally. To date
I have not died from the new virus, from melanoma,

From old age. Only one once does what Mozart did,
While most of us topple when we climb too high. Yet,
Many together accomplish miracles. Meanwhile, snow

Numbs our city and Omaha, where a daughter lives.
Meanwhile, New Orleans, sticky grey, makes love to
Another grown child. A step-daughter was supposed

To die a year ago. Sick in every imaginable way,
She has had her Covid shot, has not been out of bed
For months, lives on. Yesterday, I knew a dozen

Answers before the contestants hit their buzzers.
Michael Jordan sailed as few men sail. Daily, Barnes
Doctors perform miracles that should be impossible.

Old Man Shoveling Snow

He knows it is heart dangerous,
But, stubborn, he's doing it anyway
Because he's in better shape
Than the average eighty year old,

Who looks more like a six
Than a nine, can hardly walk,
See, think, talk, remember
Who he was in his better days.

By nature's way, all decays to dust.
Or is fired to ash like his wife.
He'll soon be nothing much, never
Was, but snow interests him now.

His shovel, polished, shining blue,
But wobbly, rickety, fits his back,
Arms, shoulders, hands. Something's
Loose in it but it works fine as he

So far in this wet, weighty snow, not
The Fifties fluff he tossed for hours
In Minnesota, where summers
He threw four tons of blacktop

Into a curber in a day. He's sweating,
Heart's beating Taps. He'd better stop,
But there are garbage cans to drag
And stairs to climb before he rests.

OLD MAN MAKES DINNER FOR HIMSELF

Peanut butter or a frozen dinner?
Frozen dinner wins again!

I think of young folk with a kitchen
Worth a hundred thousand dollars,

Never used until the epidemic.
What do I care if dinner costs me

Three whole bucks. Four minutes
In the microwave, and I am

Back to my TV. It's Friday night.
It's six pm. It's PBS News Hour.

And now, it's time, she says,
For Shields and Brooks.

But Shields (he was so good) retired
And has been replaced.

And I am almost through my day
And soon enough will be replaced.

And for His Dog

How stop this animal's demonic barking?
Perhaps, a cup of doggy heaven, dry dog food.
He's eating it. It must taste good.
Thank god! It's working.

Looks like he learned. He's bested me again,
That rat fink Chihuahua mix, fat, no good
Little turd. Now, he barks, gets paid.
I hate his grin.

Old Man Ventures Out

Tonight I'll make a salad,
Bake a piece of wild salmon
Buttered, Tajin salted,
On tin foil in a flat pan,
Add cut-up potatoes,
Broccoli dipped in olive oil,
375 degrees, twelve minutes.

Get out the mayo,
A couple baby carrots
For my conscience,
What's left of my healthy
Oatmeal cookies with pecans
And raisins. Meal for a king.

Bill, you daring epicure!

OLD MAN READS HIS OLD TESTAMENT

King David was now a very old man,
And, though they wrapped clothes round him,
He could not keep warm. His attendants said,

Let us find a young virgin for your majesty,
To attend you and take care of you;
And let her lie in your arms, sir,

And make you warm ... and they found Abishag.
Oh, my, oh, my, oh, my, what a great idea!
I wonder, what would one cost?

I can picture her. Soft and elastic, cuddly,
Warm as an electric blanket, she smells like
Ripe peaches, cinnamon, chocolate cream.

And with that image fixed in his ancient brain,
He fell fast asleep, dreamed he could skip,
Leap, run, dart, laugh through his long hair.

Lone Prairie

What an Old Man Thinks Funny

The world thinks dead serious, nasty,
Perverted, unclean, irrelevant, illegal,
The first sign of dementia. Or worse.

What could be worse? I thought it was
Comical when my poor wife, slowed
By Alzheimer's, came to breakfast

Wearing her skirt over her head,
Her legs poking out of sweater
Sleeves. For thinking that funny,

I may be damned to walking hell
Barefoot, in a mad trapper hat, mink coat,
Muffler, and balaclava. Or, worse.

Once I shot and tried to skin a squirrel.
I heard that they were good to eat.
I made a mess, squirrel pudding. Long ago,

I had the candle-lit woman of my dreams
On my sofa. She was willing. I slipped
My hand under her bra, got it stuck,

Which destroyed the mood, especially
When my first wife walked in on us,
And I tried nonchalance. Worse yet,

I think cremation's hilarious. I say
I'll be roasted, toasted, basted, grilled,
Baked, fried. Of course, I will be dead.

Old Man's Bedtime Checklist

Shower: yes,
Pee: yes
Dry off: yes

Turn down heat: yes
Lock doors, set alarm: yes
Put key on doorknob inside: yes

Dog's last walk: yes
Turn off downstairs lights: yes
Feed mice: yes

Let in feral cat: yes
Clean scratches on arm: yes
Put out food for possums: yes

Turn down covers: yes
Turn off bedside light: yes
Say goodnight to dog: yes

Say thank-you prayer: yes
For many years: yes
For healthy family: yes

For both wives: yes
For mediocre supper: yes
For sleep: yes

For waking tomorrow: yes
Say goodnight to creaking house: yes
To dancing wall shadows: yes

Ignore voice in corner: yes

Lone Prairie

WHAT AN OLD MAN FEARS

1.
You know, I used to be important
In my field, that is, not in the world.
They'd come to me with questions. We want

Your opinion on these plans. Old
Hat for me, as if I were brilliant.
I was smart, good looking; then, went bald,

Turned sixty, not the go-to guy. Can't
Go on forever. Next, the fake-gold-
-Watch goodbye. I'm weary, flatulent.

2.
It isn't just age. It's, well, my son
Doesn't respect me anymore.
He loved his daddy. I retired, earn

A good retirement. My young man wore
Me out with his competitive heart.
I tried being his friend, but he tore

Into me on little things. I'd start
Getting mad. He'd egg me on. He's gone,
Left yelling, Man, you're worthless. That hurt.

3.
I'm ignored, tell a joke,
People laugh to be nice. That's all.
My jokes are funny. Look,

Buege

I know I've grown old. Hell,
I suppose I look old. Life's stacked
Against the weak. I bowl,

Play pickle ball. In fact,
I'm fit, smarter than most, talk
Sense, dance, get no respect

What an Old Man Fears Most

1.
You are always on my mind, er,
You, yes, I know you. You died. Can't
Change it now, then, I guess I care

For her, for you, for us. I won't
Forget our, what, day. Should shut up.
Wrong more than I'm right. Then, I shan't

What? Anymore. Talk. Don't know poop.
What was I about? Write? Wears, wore
Me out, my, my to think. Daren't stop.

2.
He sits in his wheelchair and stares.
A black woman feeds, diapers him,
Drives home worn. No one really cares

For him. He's a steady job, grim
Warning we prefer to ignore
As we dance away our lives, dream

Of joys to come. Old friend, you poured
Life on fertile soil. We're aware
You had your world, but now is ours.

3.
The grown children squabble over
What he's left. Who gets the tapestry?
He doesn't care. He's dead as are

Buege

His old dog, the women he loved,
The stories he told, the scientists
He respected. Where has his time

Gone? To history, pale retelling
Of little. Soon enough, all who knew
Him will have died. He'll be no more.

Lone Prairie

Two Missouri Gardens, an Old Man, a Child

Little white butterflies in Rhonda's front garden,
A pair fluttering so in tandem they seem one,
Her garden busy with honeybees, Monarch

Butterflies, grasshoppers, insects delighting
In sun and flowers. Where have they been hiding?
Seventy-five years ago, Dad's friends carried me

Into the Steinborn's backyard morning sunshine,
Planted me in a chair beside their garden lush
With flowers, bugs, butterflies, crawlies, their hobby

Become my heaven, my every sense awake again.
Dear God, what more could I want than this
Sweet little Carthage world, this everything!

Later, recovered, I climbed aboard a bus,
Paid, walked toward the back, sat across from
A woman riding home with her groceries.

The bus driver gave me a funny look; the woman
Turned to me, asked me where I was from.
Down here, she said, white boys sit up front.

Buege

Lone Prairie

COMMENTS AND ACKNOWLEDGEMENTS

The poems in Lone Prairie are memory poems, not strictly autobiographical, but constructions using my thoughts and memories. One could almost read Sections 2 and 3 as commentary on the last poem in Section 1.

Many poems are nine lines long. I think of these short poems as a kind of picture album. The movement from photo to photo, thought to thought, memory to memory becomes the reader's construction.

A word about the composition of the nine line pieces: I enjoy the challenge a tight structure offers, controlled by syllable count and, often, terza rima rhyme or slant rhyme (aba bcb cac). I let the syllable count of the first or first and second lines control the rest of the poem.

Once again, I owe much to Daniel Wallace, an excellent editor and book architect. He has saved me from publishing some really terrible poems and has shone light on a few that at least hit their intended mark.

The poems in this book have not been previously published. After just over one hundred of my poems appeared in literary magazines, I decided I could better use my time than competing for a place in their pages with the many talented, trained young MFAs.

Northwestern University in Evanston, IL, a great university I was fortunate to attend, archives my papers. The poems in this book are published:

"Courtesy of Northwestern University Archives, William (Bill) Buege Papers"

Buege

www.ingramcontent.com/pod-product-compliance
Lightning Source LLC
Chambersburg PA
CBHW071010160426
43193CB00012B/1995